THE ALL-NITE CAFÉ

C000057479

Philip Gross was born in 1952, in Delab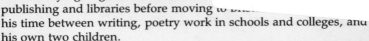
was a Displaced Person from Estonia; h
After studying English at Sussex Unive
publishing and libraries before moving to
his time between writing, poetry work in schools and colleges, and
his own two children.

   The Ice Factory was published by Faber and Faber in 1984. *Cat's Whisker* (Faber, 1987) was a Poetry Book Society Recommendation and *The Air Mines of Mistila*, a verse-fable written with Sylvia Kantaris (Bloodaxe, 1988), a Poetry Book Society Choice. He won a Gregory Award in 1981 and the National Poetry Competition in 1982; his first radio play, *Internal Affairs*, shared the prize in the BBC West of England Playwriting Competition 1986. His first collection of poems for children, *Manifold Manor*, appeared in 1989, and a novel for young people, *The Song of Gail and Fludd*, was published in spring 1991. His most recent collection of poems is *The Son of the Duke of Nowhere* (Faber, 1991). He received a major Arts Council bursary in 1989 for his work for young people.

NOTTINGHAMSHIRE COUNTY COUNCIL
LEISURE SERVICES : LIBRARIES
WITHDRAWN NOT FOR RESALE
35p

by the same author

poetry
THE ICE FACTORY
CAT'S WHISKER
THE SON OF THE DUKE OF NOWHERE

poetry for children
MANIFOLD MANOR

fiction for children
THE SONG OF GAIL AND FLUDD

PHILIP GROSS
The All-Nite Café

Nottinghamshire County Council

821.914 GRO

34502065

Leisure Services/Libraries

faber and faber
LONDON · BOSTON

First published in 1993
by Faber and Faber Limited
3 Queen Square London WC1N 3AU

Photoset by Wilmaset Ltd, Birkenhead, Wirral
Printed in Great Britain by
Cox & Wyman Ltd, Reading, Berkshire

All rights reserved

© Philip Gross, 1993

Philip Gross is hereby identified as author of this work in accordance
with the Copyright, Designs and Patents Act 1988

*This book is sold subject to the condition that it shall not, by way of trade
or otherwise, be lent, resold, hired out or otherwise circulated without the
publisher's prior consent in any form of binding or cover other than that
in which it is published and without a similar condition including
this condition being imposed on the subsequent purchaser.*

CIP data for this book is available from
the British Library

ISBN 0 571 16753 5

Contents

Night Light

You dreamed you were falling? Good!
Where did you fall to and what did you find?

*Advice from the elders of the Senoi people
of North East Burma*

Full fathom five thy father lies;
  Of his bones are corals made:
Those are pearls that were his eyes:
  Nothing of him that doth fade,
But doth suffer a sea-change
Into something rich and strange.

Shakespeare, *The Tempest*

On Hungerford Bridge

It's the end of the day,

the middle of the city . . .
   On the long iron footbridge
     all the light is grey,

too heavy for the sky
   to hold. The heavy river
     sluices it away.

There's a shudder of rain,
   then stillness, one wide puddle,
     and I'm walking on the same

mud-swirling clouds
   I'm walking under, out
     to where he squats: a stray

man bundled in a blanket.
   He twirls high wheedling jigs
     from a whistle and won't say

Thank-you-kindly-sir. He frowns
   at the twists in the tune
     and doesn't stop to weigh

my thin chink in his sodden
   nest of coins. The toll.
     And if I didn't pay?

The other side I reach might
   seem to be no different, but . . .
     Look back. He's gone. It's night.

Lock up Your Clocks

The grandfather clock in the hall
like a perfect butler stands aside
by day. If it speaks, it's only,
tactfully, to fill a silence.
  Until night-time . . .

Then bury your head if you will
in your pillow. You can't help but hear
that weighty footfall through
deserted rooms downstairs. Clocks
  bide their time.

The video recorder flickers green
beneath the TV table. It's alert
as a spider, busy netting dreams
from the airwaves while we're sleeping.
  Lights-out time

and everywhere and nowhere rise
small clockwork cries, squeaky-creaky
like rain-forest frogs or, digital,
the brittle whirr of insect wings.
  Bad time

to be awake. The ticker in your chest
picks up the threat. The night's alive
with tapped-out messages on frequencies
we can't quite catch, or won't, or not
  in time –

like yellow teeth, like claws at work
on the bars of the cage . . . A scratching
at the cell wall . . . Stropping of long knives,
short whispers: *Brothers, soon will come
  the time* . . .

The stroke of one. The town-hall clock.
Far off, another answers, slightly
  out of time.

For One Night Only

The deadbeat circus
rolls up on the hard edge of town.

They're sledge-hammering stakes in, raising
cinder dust and thistledown.

Now they've run up a slack flounce of tent.
A man barks at the moon.

They've nailed their colours to the sky
just as it darkens. Two bald clowns

come flatfoot, fly-postering everything
that can't get away. The show goes on.

And on. Long past bedtime,
the stilt-walker stalks through the streets,

face level with your bedroom window.
In the morning, someone will be gone.

At the All-Nite Café

Come on down down down. Could be any old street.
Don't know where you're going you just follow your feet
down down. There are people you'd never dream you'd meet
    in the cold light of day.
    See, they've saved you a seat.
It's got your number on it and you don't have to pay
    at the All-Nite Café.

It's not a tavern but a cavern, not a café but a cave.
There's nothing on the menu but *Whatever You Crave*.
Try the steak *à la* Dracula, with gravy from the grave
    as the band begins to play.
    The singer needs a shave.
Or could he be a werewolf? He's howling anyway
    in the All-Nite Café.

See those Hell's Angel cowboys with their longhorn bikes,
their bad black leather and chains and skulls and spikes.
They're drinking pink milkshakes with a couple of Vik-
    -ings. It's always the way.
    Everyone does what he likes –
all the secret little wishes that they don't dare say –
    at the All-Nite Café.

See the black-robed monk heating something in the fire
with a nice schoolteacher who just called in to enquire
about the right sort of instruments to use on the choir
    to get that top A
    Whatever you desire!
Thumbscrews? The rack? She'll make them squeal OK
    at the All-Nite Café.

It's the superheroes' social club. They come for a chat
like old folk do. Even Superman is running to fat.
And Robin's voice is breaking as he says: *Gee, Bat-*
man, your hair's gone grey.
And here comes Postman Pat.
He's been given the sack and his cat has gone astray
at the All-Nite Café.

It's like a hundred crossed lines on a disconnected phone,
like a rush-hour in a jumble sale and yet you're all alone
and every single stranger could be somebody you've known
somewhere before, as they
smile: *Welcome home!*
They'll always be waiting at the end of the day
at the All-Nite Café.

There's a non-stop cabaret

at the All-Nite Café.

(Just step this way . . .

Dirge for Unwin

Uncle Unwin
lived unwed,
died unmourned,
our tears unshed,
his chin unshaved,
his soul unsaved,
his feet unwashed,
his cat unfed,

uncouth, unkempt,
no cuff unfrayed,
his floor unswept,
his bed unmade,
ungenerous,
unkind to us,
the undertaker's
bill unpaid

until
       his will,
found undercover,
left untold wealth
to an unknown lover.
It's so unfair.
We were unaware:
even nobodies count
on one another.

Ring of Gold

I saw a goldfinch in the garden
on a cold grey day.
One? One is luck,
Grandmother used to say.

I saw a goldfish in a pond
mouthing words that made no sense.
(And a goldfinch in the garden . . .) *Two?*
Grandmother said. *Coincidence.*

I saw the gold tooth glinting
in the postman's grin.
(And a goldfish and a goldfinch . . .) *Three?*
Three is a message. Take it in.

It was a packet from a long-lost uncle
postmarked Ecuador.
He found a gold mine. (Gold tooth,
goldfish, goldfinch . . .) Four.

Four is a warning. Fools
let numbers rule their lives.
He lost the lot at cards, all
but a small gold locket. *Five's*

a parting. (Mine, tooth, fish, bird,
locket) . . . and a twist of fine
gold hair inside. No picture.
(With the locket and the mine,

tooth, fish and bird, that's . . .) *Six*
is a mystery. A curl
like a question mark between two lovers
who can never leave the garden, the girl

always lifting a hand to her hair,
something catching the sun – a ring,
not the boy's (*Seven? Seven's the end.*)
like the flash of a goldfinch's wing.

To See a Ghost

To see a ghost
is to wait in a train
as another pulls in
the opposite way

and through the glass
only inches from yours
a face you almost
know from years

and years ago
stares back. Those eyes
meet yours. You blink
at each other's surprise

and see the *Oh!*
on each other's lips
as one train shudders
and begins to slip

away so smoothly
that neither can tell
which is moving,
which is still,

and who's going up,
who down, the line
and who's running on,
who out, of time.

Eclipse

I sat up half the night
to spy on them. The moon
tipped the earth a slow
wink. Shutters clicked.
It was midnight up there too.

Our shadow could not quite
put out the glow. Dark
pearl . . . Hot copper cooling . . .
Or the dull flush
of a boozer's nose.

So I'm told. All I saw
was a fug of buff streetlight.
The city snugged down in its fumes
like a slob in a duvet –
no moon,

an eclipse of the night.

The Iron Sweep

(A Victorian Master Sweep's trade sign,
now in Cheltenham Museum.)

Granfer Grimstone,
iron sweep,
walks in his hundred-
year-long-sleep.

Grass dies blackened
where he sat
in his cast-iron coat.
His stovepipe hat

is a chimney smirched
with smoke and smut.
His eye-holes glow
from the fire in his gut.

He hunts for the time
that's good and dead.
He's just the shell
some live thing shed.

He walks and walks
earth's clinker crust
and dreams the only
dream he dreams
                    of rust.

Multi Storey

'Level 13. Don't forget. By the car,'
　　they said. 'Don't be late.'
　　　　But you are.

You punch the buttons one by one.
　　No hum. The lift is dead.
　　　　So you run

up twist on twist of empty stair,
　　can't stop, till the walls
　　　　spin – bare

bone concrete splashed with beer
　　or worse and spray-scrawls:
　　　　WE WUZ ERE.

JEN 4 BAZ. Levels 8 . . . 9 . . . 10 . . .
　　13 . . . Through the door, look.
　　　　Look again:

it's wrong. Try one flight up. One more,
　　up or down, no difference.
　　　　Every floor,

it hits you with a breath of chill
　　and stale fumes, is 13.
　　　　And all so still.

The roof above, the floor beneath
　　are closing on the light
　　　　like teeth

as you hunt down line on silent line
　　of cars like rusting waggons
　　　　in a worked-out mine.

And inside every windscreen there are eyes
　　as cold as mirrors, with a look
　　　　you recognize

from Sunday snarl-ups queuing for the coast.
  They stare you back as if
    you were the ghost:

Dads grim as captains in the driving seat,
  Mums tight-lipped at their side.
    Their eyes never meet.

The back of their heads is all the kids see
  blocking out where they're going,
    that's patiently

waiting round the next bend out of sight
  as Dad puts his foot down. Squeal
    of brakes or fright

and *Wake up!* Just in time. These stories
  always end like that,
    don't they?
                      Sure,

  all but one.

Who-man

Mud-man mask with a snaggle of teeth:
>   *who?*
Sawn-off stocking-head knuckle-faced thief:
>   *who?*
Death-mask of gold in a high king's tomb
  and the mask of the skull that grins beneath:

>   *but whose*
>   *are the eyes,*
>   *the eyes inside?*
>   *Can they see you?*

Hallowe'en fang-face trick or treat:
>   *who?*
Eye-holes snipped in your parents' sheet:
>   *who?*
Night inside and the thud of your blood
  like a skin-tight drum begins to beat:

>   *but whose*
>   *are the eyes,*
>   *the eyes inside,*
>   *the eyes that hide?*
>   *It can't be you.*

Visor of a biker or the riot police:
>   *who?*
Whiteface clown dripping tears of grease:
>   *who?*
Images reflected in a film star's shades.
  A false friend's smile. (That's last, not least.)

>   *And whose*
>   *are the eyes,*
>   *the eyes inside,*
>   *the eyes that hide*
>   *in hurt or hate or fear or pride?*
>   *What do they want? And who?*

The Ace of Strange

Playing Patience with yourself
on a flat wet evening
that's been going on for ever.
It's a sad and stupid game.
It just won't come out
and the same goes for you.
There's just one card left.
    Please say
    it's . . . Yes?
    No way.
    Unless . . .

Where there's a giggle in the class
that nobody started
and the teacher goes bananas
but no one can explain;
when there's a hush in the room
like an angel passing over;
when a goose walks on your grave . . .
    Who spoke?
    Not me.
    No joke.
    Maybe . . .

No, it isn't
what he is, it's what
he isn't that's his business. It's
his isn't-   *what-he-is-ness.*
He's the voice   *that says* **All Change.**
He's the space   *in the place you could*
have sworn   *you saw a face in.*
There's no stranger
kind of stranger
than

the Ace
of
Strange.

When the flags went limp
and the crowd fell silent
and the grey dictator knew
things would never be the same,
you can search all the newsreels
for the first man to stop cheering.
See that blur in the background?
  Could it be?
  Don't know.
  Search me.
  Although . . .

Playing Poker in the dark
with that charming Mr Horniman . . .
We've lost our shirts and our souls.
Let's raise the stakes again
till the last card flips
and we're hoping it's the joker
or we'll all go up in smoke.
  Double or quits.
  Sink or swim.
  Touch and go. It's
  him!

     No, it isn't
    what he is, it's what
   he isn't that's his business. It's
  his isn't-   *what-he-is-ness.*
  He's the voice   *that says* **All Change**.
  He's the space   *in the place you could*
  have sworn   *you saw a face in.*
     There's no stranger
    kind of stranger. He's
    the cheat, the chop-
    and-changer. He's
   the baby in the manger.
   He's an ever-
    present danger.
     He's

    the Ace
    of
    Strange.

Fighting Fantasy

Thus the Black Horde of Morgravain
faced the pale Prince Albigon
across the snowswept Plain
of . . .

      Page one hundred and six,
as I fumble it, damn!
slips and nicks
my fingertip, so
quick the pain
seems to come from no-
where till a garnet bead
leaks, *drip*
on the page.
                  Read
on now: how the black
ranks and the white
drew back
aghast and froze.

There on the snow between them bloomed
one blood-red rose.

Mirror, Mirror

TODDLER AT HIS PARENTS' MIRROR

Looking up and
up and up to
me gives him
a funny feeling:
Why do grown-
up mirrors
need to show
such a lot
of ceiling?

A DEEP WELL LOOKS BACK AT A BOY

I show
him his face
very small and alone
in the dark. Is that what
makes him throw
a stone?

TWO FROM A FAIRGROUND HALL OF MIRRORS

I
'll
str-
-etch
you like
a stick
of tof-
-fee till
you cry:
STOP!

I'll huff and I'll puff you out like bubble gum.
You'll laugh till you . . .

Pop!

JOYRIDER AND A REAR-VIEW MIRROR

He uses me to slick his hair,
dead cool, doing 90, instead
of noticing the sign behind –
POLICE – or the corner ahead.

BLIND DATE

She loves him . . . Loves him not . . . Loves me,
  her mirror, best of all.

She came back late tonight. With him.
  She faced me to the wall.

DRUNKEN UNCLE IN THE GENTS AT THE BODGER'S ARMS
You're only as old
  as you feel, me lad,
    eh?
      He's attempting
    to straighten
                    his tie
    and his moustache. (I
      don't reply.)
        There's life
                    in the old
            dog yet . . .
              But he can't
      look himself in the eye.

A SILENT FILM STAR'S POCKET MIRROR
                    She
                  looked
                and looked
              away. She locked me
              in my jewelled case.
              I guard the fading
                  after-image
                      of her
                      face.

TWO MIRRORS LEFT ACCIDENTALLY FACING EACH OTHER
[Both, at once:] WHERE AM I?!?!?

Night School

Somehow I'm back, at the back of the class
behind the same old heads and shoulders.
    But it's dark.

only a slantwise rod of moonlight on the floor
at the feet of the figure in black who creaks
    chalk on the board.

And whatever it was we were meant to be learning
I can't for the life of me think. So long ago . . .
    Now he turns

and just as I'm going to have to see his face
he sinks with his head in his hands. His script
    is faint as spider's lace:

I cannot teach you any more.

In front of each of us, a sealed envelope . . .
Our end-of-term reports. It's so hard to resist.
    'Do not open

on pain of . . .' Billy next to me, he's eased
his open. He slips the paper out. He squints.
    He drops it. *Please,*

Sir – his voice is an old man's whisper – *May I
be excused?* The paper lies there: 'William
    Hope. Passed away

May 13th, 2036, aged 55. RIP.'
It's a clip from *The Times*. So we know
    what the teacher means

as he looks up with his hollow eyes, his sunken jaw:

I cannot teach you any more.

Growler

Like a toad
beneath a suddenly
flipped stone

huffed up
as if about
to sing (but no

sound comes)
yes, it was me.
I was the one

who cracked the bell
of everyone's *Hey-
Ring-A-Ding-Ding-*

Sweet-Lovers-Love-the . . .
'Stop!' Miss Carver
clapped her hands.

'Which one of you's
the Growler?' No one
breathed. 'Very well.

Sing on.' And she leaned
very close
all down the line till

'Stop!'
She was as small as me
(aged eight)

but sour and sixty,
savage for the love
of her sweet music

I was curdling.
'You!
How *dare* you?

Out!' Down the echoing
hall, all eyes on me . . .
My one big solo.

She died last year.
I hope somebody sang.
Me, I'm still growling.

People-in-Cars

People-in-cars are ugly.
The big ones sag baggy as toads.
The small ones sit up smugly
   like prize porkers on their way to market.

People-in-cars ignore
the rest of us. We're a boring old film
they've seen before
   and can change with a flick of the gearstick.

People-in-cars are gross.
They have horns and are noisy and deaf.
At traffic lights they pick their noses
   and sing with their stereos, flat.

Young people-in-cars demand
things with menaces: sweets and crisps
and double jumbo burgers *and*
   an extra-thick milkshake. Then they're sick.

Parent people-in-cars go stiff
and turn their backs and drive,
drive, drive as if
   by going faster they might just escape.

They're all monsters, half human, half car.
They go in herds and hate
each other. This has gone too far.
   The time has come to say it straight:
   there ought to be a law against them stamp them out clamp down
                    exterminate exterminate . . .

                    (*Other* people in cars, that is.)

History Lesson

First, one
in the crowd puts the eye on you –
a nod to number two

who gets the message
and flips back something side-
long, something snide

that everybody hears
but you. Soon three or four
are in it. They'll make sure

you catch the steel
glint of the snigger they wear
like a badge. And there

come five or six
together, casual, shouldering in
around you with a single grin

and nothing you say
seems to reach them at all.
The badmouthings they call

mean only this:
they want to scratch. You are the itch.
A thousand years stand by, hissing *Witch!*

Nigger! Yid!
All you hear is silence lumbered
shut around you. And the ten or hundred

looking on
look on. They are learning not to see.
The bell rings, too late. Already

this is history.

Poetic Licence

Crack! A racket of muskets. The echoes rebound.
Torches spatter the dark. It's like a battle underground.
   Bats scatter in rubbery panic like . . . well,
    what can you say but: bats out of Hell?
      And crash! a stalactite is downed.

Another! Twenty thousand years they've grown
drip by drip, like . . . waterfalls of stone?
   Accusing fingers? No. He knows it's
    not quite right. But he's a poet. Poets
      can't leave things alone.

So he speaks to the bishop who speaks to his friend
the colonel, who laughs: if poetry's at stake, he'll lend
   some dragoons, eh what, tally-ho,
    they'll shoot the beggars down. And so
      they do. Now the poet will send

for an ox-cart to rumble and trundle the lot
to his modest dwelling by the Thames (for he's not
   a vandal, he's a man renowned
    for good taste). In the grounds
      he'll build a little grotto

which two hundred years later will be blown to bits
by a Luftwaffe bomb off-target from the Blitz
   while the sky over blacked-out London glows
    like a cave by torchlight. Which just goes
      to show: where poets miss

the point, the real world scores direct hits.

This is a true story. The poet was Alexander Pope (1688–1744).
The cave was Wookey Hole. The Second World War really happened.

Drop

At the start I was swaddled in sea.
Mother moon moved the mass of us monthly.
We were well. I was one with her will.

Then the strong sun smiled on me. I swooned.
His love lifted me like lark song and I let it.
I was cloud, carried on. Over country I climbed.

Here, too heavy for heaven to hold me,
I felt myself forming, then fell fierce and free,
rattling roofs in a rage, in grey gutters gushing.

Dashed down drains with the dirt and the dregs,
scum of sump-oil, I sank where the sun could not see,
running off at a roadside to wrangle with root-hairs.

Worms were workers of wonders with me when
in the grit and the gravel I gave grass its growth.
So I sank down exhausted, surrendered to silence.

Last came the long years locked in limestone,
cold and calm. I come out at last clear,
purged of the past and its poisons, purified . . .

> . . . and here the drop, before it lets
> go and its own reflection
> in the cave pool leaps
> to meet it, hesitates.
> Hangs. Shivers. Any
> moment. Any
> moment

> *NOW*

Daughter of the Sea

bog seeper
moss creeper
growing restless
getting steeper

trickle husher
swish and rusher
stone leaper
splash and gusher

foam flicker
mirror slicker
pebble pusher
boulder kicker

still pool
don't be fooled
shadow tricker
keeping cool

leap lunger
crash plunger
free fall
with thunder under

idle winder
youth behind her
little wonder
daily grinder

garbage binner
dump it in her
never mind her
dog's dinner

plastic bagger
old lagger
oil skinner
wharf nagger

cargo porter
weary water
tide dragger
long-lost daughter

of the sea
the sea the sea
has caught her
up in its arms and set her free

Sargasso

I
was
born
free in
hanging
gardens.
  My cradle
  of weed
  was swung
  beneath
  a green
  canopy
warmed by
father sun
rocked by
mother sea
aṣ it was
in the be-
  ginning
  when time
  too was
  young.

I
dreamed
of land
before
  I saw it,
  tasted
  sweet
  water
  before
I met it
head on,
  funnelled
  up rivers,
  slipping
into streams,
squirming
  up brooks,
  the snugger
  the safer.
Every crack
that had
water to
breathe
  was home
  to me.

I
was
fine
as a hair
and clear
  as glass.
A current
ruffled us.
Millions
set out,
twisting
  east two
  thousand
  miles.
  Millions
were lost.
The Gulf
Stream was
our only
teacher
and a
bitter
one.

I
lodged
in a ditch
between
cool slabs
of peat.
I lay
like a warrior
in a tomb.
Time slept
at my side.
Catch me now,
you'll rue
the day. Old
eels won't
die. I knew
one chopped
into three-
inch chunks
but her jaws
still bit
the hand
that caught
her. Hah!
It's an
old tale
but I
like
it.

I
dream
these days
of green
light, a world
without walls
or floor. Wind,
rain tonight,
a full moon
and the air
is wet enough
to breathe.
This ditch
can't hold me
now. I'll steer
by the smell
of the sea. Land
creatures, if
you see me
coming, step
aside. I'm going
home. I warn
you. Don't
stand
in my
way.

Note:
All the eels of
Europe are spawned
in the floating weed
of the
Sargasso Sea.
They swim
the Atlantic
twice:
once as young
fish to reach
our shores,
and back at
the end
of their lives
to spawn and
die.

Tales from the Dark Continent

You're lost. This is the unexplored
interior
where it's always the hour before dawn.
What's that? There!

Just an inkling: a jittery
creep with a quivering snout.
It's alarmed by the *flunk!* of a wobbly
throwing itself about

in search of little niggles
which in turn
nag away at the ground for the wriggle
of a worried squirm.

A scaredycat scurries
through the quease. He looks a fright.
He cringes at a flurry
of small flinches taking flight

in the qualm trees. He turns pale
at the whimper of a squeam.
At a flutter of jitters, he quails.
Then suddenly, a scream . . .

It's a habdab!
And everything rushes
gibbering and jabbering
through the hysteria bushes.

Families of heebiejeebies
clutch their little horrors.
They hug their knocking knees and freeze
as a hoohah roars
                    and the clock
                        strikes
                            four.

Sea Changes

1

VOYAGE TO THE EDGE OF SLEEP

    Flat calm.
The sea is the floor of a darkened ballroom
polished to a mirror. But the ball is over.
    All the guests are gone.

    And even
if your boat could move there's nowhere
to be nearer to or further from.
    It's then

    the eyes
like headlamps in a fog, the eyes
of dream fish moon up watching,
    hungry. Slick

    backs nudge
the surface as you scatter in
the dry crumbs of your day. A gush
    and thrash of fins

    but silently
and as the ripples settle
you've forgotten
    everything –

          how you came
            where you're bound
           who you are and
                   then . . .

2

GHOST FORESTS

. . . you see it all
in a cool glow like a fridge door
left ajar

in an empty house at midnight.
Amazonian forests.
There they are,

drowned but alive,
more alive than up here.
They've lost their memory

of being slashed and burned.
They're safe now,
breathing water easily.

Quick fish like glints
of tigers' eyes blink
into cover. In the silt

of a clearing, a bulldozer
noses like a pond snail.
Two male lobsters stilt

their courtship dance
around a comfortably
rusting excavator.

It responds with a quivering
bob and dip
of its claw.

The souls of the woodcutters
put down their chainsaws
and spread the wings

they never knew they had.
The forest takes them up
and up. They sing.

3

THE SUBMARINES' GRAVEYARD

A scuttled submarine lies at its ease
growing long hippy tresses of weed.
No one shouts *Get your hair cut.*
Urchins, brittle-stars, anemones

are the medals it's won. The armour-plate
is barnacles. They sift the water patiently.
The poison in its heart decays:
Ten thousand years? They'll wait.

Meanwhile sailors of several nations
rummage through their Davy-Jones's-
locker-room of wreckage, sorting out
their badges of rank, sea-boots and bones.

The current keeps mixing them up.
(Which country expects which man
to do what duty?) Even when
an admiral collects enough

gold braid to issue a command,
his speech-bubbles wobble up, perfectly
empty and never quite round:
the same in every language, silvery

balloons above a fairground crowd.

4

SHEEP DIP

A flock of sheep,
slightly dazed from the slaughterhouse,
  bob by, meek

  as dumplings in a stew.
Their dolphin guide explains *again*: she
  once was a landlubber, too.

  Now look at her –
sleek and free! All it takes
  is a bit of flair

  and evolution. Easy!
Now, who's going to take the plunge?
  Slip off your fleece!

5

A BAD CASE OF FISH

A chip-shop owner's in the dock
on a charge of assault and battery.
The monkfish takes the oath:
So help me cod . . .

The courtroom's packed with lost soles.
The crabby judge can't find his plaice
or read the prosecution's whiting.
And what sort of fish is a saveloy, anyway?

The young skates are getting bored.
They start skateboarding down the aisles.
The scampi scamper to and fro.
The eels are dancing congers.

But the case is cut and dried.
It's all wrapped up. (Just look
in the evening paper.) Next,
the Krayfish twins . . .

6

ON THE SIDELINES

Who are these – stooping and shuffling
like old men in black plastic macs
   in an endless bus queue
     on a rainy day?

The buses which splash by and never stop
have drivers with the face of tanker captains
   who threw the switch
     to flush the tank

to spill the slick which was the death
of these little old men of the sea:
   puffin, cormorant, shag,
     gull, gannet, guillemot . . .

7

TIME AND TIDE

There are faces you know
   but the sea
has done something to time. Here's one you recognize

from old photographs – grandfather
   as a boy,
with long socks and a cap he flings so high

that the wind (or the tide) floats it free
   and away:
a jellyfish. The tide turns; so does time

and there are your parents, young
   and clumsy
on their first night out. The twinkles in their eye

escape as quick bright fishes.
   (A shark-shape,
shadow of a warship, passes through the small fry.

   All the glints go out but one.)

8

THE FAT AND THE THIN

There's a city down there
    struggling,
stuck in a endless rush hour.
It's business as usual –
    grumbling, troubling –

though the straight streets
    (gritting, grinding)
keep dissolving into green lanes
more the shape of ocean currents'
    winding.

Still the people soldier on,
    huffing, waddling.
Some wear their own importance
like a Mayor's gold chain.
    All their bothering

weights them down. See them
    stumbling
on till worked out, slimmed
down one by one they slip
    wriggling, tumbling

out of their bonds, and rise,
    scarcely believing,
light at last, to join the shoals
of weightless people: all the hungry ones,
    already swooping, weaving,

skinny children born
    into short lives of dying
and the parents who carried them
on through the dust and the drought,
    all rise here, flying.

9

FINALE

And a whale, just one
bag-lady of a humpback passes, hung

above it all. She is grey
and shapeless as a raincloud. Far away,

mumbling old melodies,
she's in a dream where seven weary seas

link hands as before
and come out on the glittering dance floor

for her solo. All
the world of water hushes, like the Albert Hall.

Night Light

When I was small
each night
was a bottomless ocean.
But I had a pale pink
plastic lighthouse
with a one-watt bulb,
enough to tip its wink
to the brass of the doorknob
like a ship
passing far out to sea.
And high above it all
on a safe shore
was the lookout: me.

And now
I'm told that space
is truly bottomless
and endless and the sun
is a tiny nightlight
glinting sometimes
on nine crumbs
of rock or ice
and there's nowhere anyone
can stand above it all.
Hello? Can anybody
hear me? I'm
so small.

Song of the Punk Mermaids

One night as I
sailed on the deep
a terrible cry
roused me from sleep.
You can say I was dreaming, you can say I was drunk,
but I could have sworn it said: *Hi,*
                                        I'm Lady Di.
(Di Oxin to you.) I'm a mermaid punk.

They were sitting on the end of an outfall pipe.
They couldn't sing in tune, but the words were pretty ripe:
Yeah, we're Lady Di Oxin and Jenny the Junk.
Stuff your madrigals and ballads. We're singing punk!

Our hair's bright green, it just went that way.
There's heavy metal in the sea, there's acid in the rain
and the oil rigs bang away like disco funk.
It's an all-night rave for Lady Di Oxin,
                        Nora Noxious
                        and Jenny the Junk.
Stuff your lullabies and love songs. We're singing punk!

There once was a lad, ran away to sea,
as rough and tough and hunky as a sailor boy should be.
One look at us, ran back to land to be a monk.
Was it something we sang? Lady Di Oxin,
                        Nora Noxious,
                        Scumbelina
                        and Jenny the Junk.
Stuff your hornpipes and your shanties. We're singing punk!

You think we're offensive? Yeah, we got bad taste
It really makes us spit, this industrial waste.
Dab a bit behind your ears and you smell like a skunk.
Good, eh? It's all the rage for Lady Di Oxin,
                              Nora Noxious,
                              Scumbelina,
                              Toxic Tessa
                              and Jenny the Junk.
Stuff your carols and cantatas. We're singing punk!

So come all you saucy sailors, any Tom or Dick or Gerry,
on your tanker or container ship or roll-on-roll-off ferry.
You'll see us in your dreams as you're lying in your bunk.
Hope it makes you seasick. We're Lady Di Oxin,
                              Nora Noxious,
                              Scumbelina,
                              Toxic Tessa,
                              Effluenza
                              and Jenny the Junk.
Stuff your pretty little ditties. We're singing punk!

Small Dawn Song

This is just to say Thank You

to the tick
   of the downstairs clock
      like a blind man's stick
         tap-tip on through the dark

to the lone
   silly blackbird who sang
      before dawn when no one
         should have been listening

to the wheeze
   and chink of the milk float
      like an old nightwatchman clinking keys
         and clearing his throat

      Six o'clock and all's well
      Six o'clock and all's well

The night's been going on
           so long
           so long

This is just to say Thank You.